DINOSAUR INFOSAURUS

DINOSAUR
BONES AND FOSSILS

Katie Woolley

WAYLAND
www.waylandbooks.co.uk

First published in Great Britain in 2019
by Wayland

Editor: Elise Short
Design: Peter Clayman

HB ISBN: 978 1 5263 1117 7
PB ISBN: 978 1 5263 1118 4

10 9 8 7 6 5 4 3 2 1

Wayland, an imprint of
Hachette Children's Group
Part of Hodder and Stoughton
Carmelite House
50 Victoria Embankment
London EC4Y 0DZ

An Hachette UK Company
www.hachette.co.uk
www.hachettechildrens.co.uk

Printed and bound in China

Picture acknowledgements:
All images curtesy of Shutterstock except:
Dreamstime main images: 12-13; 14-15; 16-17; 20-21; 22-
23; Alamy: Pictorial Press Ltd: 28r; Getty: Karl Gehring/
The Denver Post: 29br; Getty: Nicky Loh: 29bl;
Getty: Bettmann: 29tl; Martin Williams: 29tr;
Martin Bustamente illustrations: 4-5; 6-7.

CONTENTS

THE WORLD OF THE DINOSAURS

Dinosaurs lived between **245 and 66 million years ago** (mya), during the **Mesozoic Era**. They successfully ruled Earth for more than 150 million years. Palaeontologists learn about these prehistoric creatures from the **remains** they left behind. These remains are called **fossils**.

The first dinosaur to be described scientifically was **Megalosaurus** [MEG-ah-low-sore-us] in 1824.

New fossils are being found all the time. Palaeontologists are uncovering about **50 new species** of dinosaur a year. That's an average of nearly **one a week**!

Scientists have ways of **identifying** dinosaur bones. For example, they might recognise the **shape** of the bone or tooth from a previous fossil find.

Meat-eaters had **sharp teeth** for tearing and cutting through flesh, while plant-eaters had **flatter teeth** for grinding down plants and trees.

New **technology** means scientists can learn more and more about dinosaurs from their fossil remains. For example **CT scans**, which use X-rays to **reconstruct** living or fossilised things in three dimensions using computers, are being used to **look inside** dinosaur skulls.

A recent CT scan of a **Tyrannosaurus rex** [tie-RAN-oh-sore-us rex] revealed it had large internal sense organs. This mighty meat-eater had a great sense of smell!

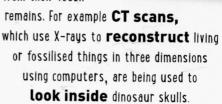

BONE FOSSILS

Fossils finds can be split into **bone fossils** and **trace fossils** (see pages 8–9). Bone fossils tell us about an animal's body. They are the most common kind of fossil and include body parts such as teeth, bones, claws and, more rarely, soft body tissue.

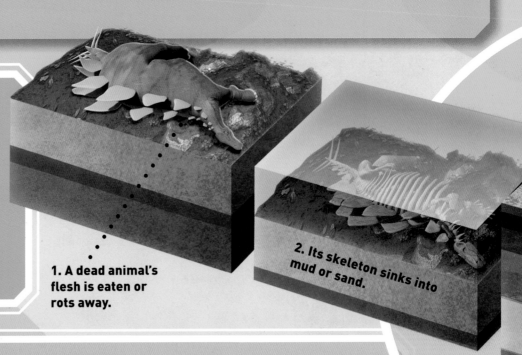

Most dead animals do not become fossils. Usually, when an animal dies its body **decays**, and **breaks down** but occasionally the right conditions means the process of **fossilisation** can begin:

1. A dead animal's flesh is eaten or rots away.

2. Its skeleton sinks into mud or sand.

Bone fossils can be split into four categories:

Articulated skeleton An almost complete skeleton with its bones still joined together.

Associated skeleton When bones are found to be from the same animal but have been broken apart.

Isolated bone
One bone, such as a thigh bone (femur).

Float A piece of bone.

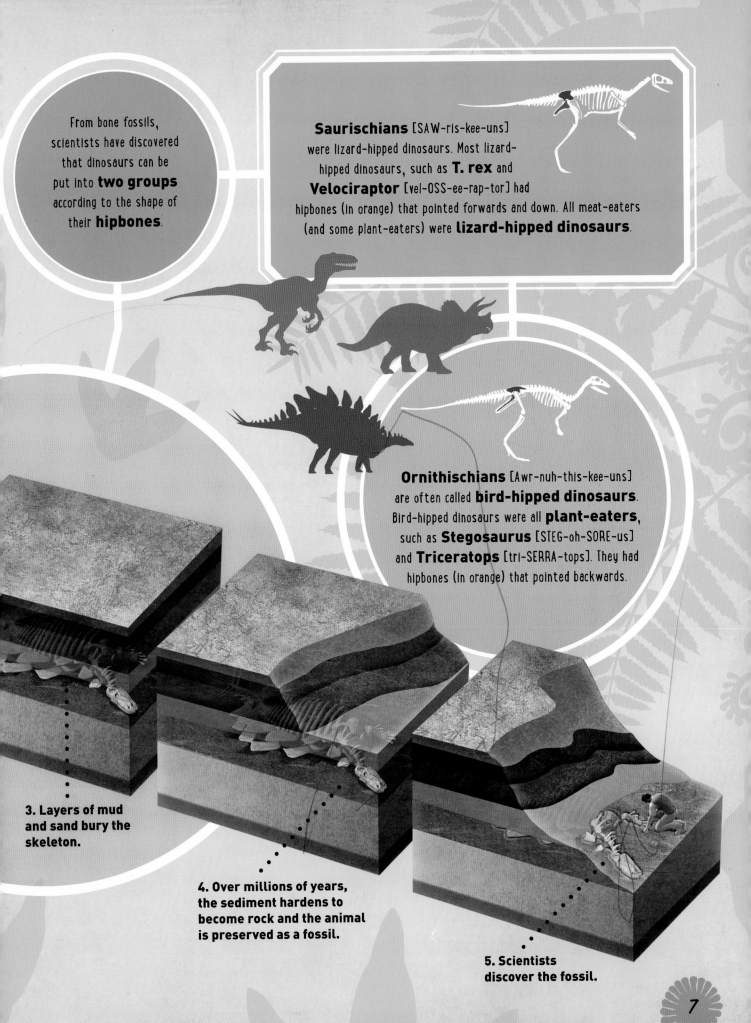

From bone fossils, scientists have discovered that dinosaurs can be put into **two groups** according to the shape of their **hipbones**.

Saurischians [SAW-ris-kee-uns] were lizard-hipped dinosaurs. Most lizard-hipped dinosaurs, such as **T. rex** and **Velociraptor** [vel-OSS-ee-rap-tor] had hipbones (in orange) that pointed forwards and down. All meat-eaters (and some plant-eaters) were **lizard-hipped dinosaurs**.

Ornithischians [Awr-nuh-this-kee-uns] are often called **bird-hipped dinosaurs**. Bird-hipped dinosaurs were all **plant-eaters**, such as **Stegosaurus** [STEG-oh-SORE-us] and **Triceratops** [tri-SERRA-tops]. They had hipbones (in orange) that pointed backwards.

3. Layers of mud and sand bury the skeleton.

4. Over millions of years, the sediment hardens to become rock and the animal is preserved as a fossil.

5. Scientists discover the fossil.

7

TRACE FOSSILS

Occasionally the fossils of **footprints** or **dinosaur poo** are found. These are known as 'trace fossils' because they help us learn about a dinosaur's **behaviour**.

Trace fossils formed when a **footprint** or **dinosaur poo** was left in soft mud or sand and quickly dried before it could be washed away. It was then covered in layers of rock, sand and mud which **preserved** the fossil.

Fossilised tracks can reveal if a dinosaur walked on two feet or four, how quickly it moved and if it lived alone or in herds.

Fossilised poo, called **coprolite**, can help palaeontologists learn what dinosaurs ate. Coprolites are very rare because dinosaur poo would have usually been washed away quickly.

One of the **largest** dinosaur **coprolites** ever found was 44 cm long and 13 cm wide! That's about the same length as two footballs side by side. This enormous poo contained **bone** that the dinosaur had eaten, so scientists think this coprolite came from a large meat-eating dinosaur, such as **T. rex**.

Coprolites from dinosaurs from the Cretaceous period (146 to 65 mya) such as Maiasaura [my-ah-SORE-ah] have been found with **small burrows** in them. Creatures that fed on the poo, such as **dung beetles**, probably made the holes.

In 2018, researchers from the University of Edinburgh found dozens of **footprints** on the Isle of Skye in Scotland. Some of these footprints belonged to huge **sauropods**. Each track was up to 70 cm wide – that's as big as a **car tyre**!

Theropods left tracks at the site, too. The footprints crossed up and down across ground that would have once been **water**, suggesting these dinosaurs often moved in and out of the shallows.

In 2005, the world's **smallest dinosaur footprint**, just 1.8 cm long, was found on the Isle of Skye but scientists aren't sure which dinosaur it belonged to.

North America has been a hot spot for fossil hunters. More than **400 fossils** have been found in Alberta, **Canada** alone, including **Albertosaurus** [al-BERT-oh-sore-us], **Ankylosaurus** [an-KIE-loh-sore-us] and **Troodon** [TROH-oh-don].

One dinosaur bone bed in Utah, **USA**, is home to over **10,000 bones**. Some of these bones are believed to be from plant-eaters who became **trapped in the mud** at the edge of a lake. They attracted the attention of predators who also became trapped.

North America

DINOSAURS AROUND THE WORLD

During the time of the dinosaurs, Earth began as one big land mass called **Pangaea**. Over the **Mesozoic Era**, Pangaea began to break apart. As it **split**, dinosaurs moved across the land. Pangaea became Earth's seven **continents** and dinosaur **fossils** have been found on every one.

South America

There have been some important recent dinosaur discoveries in **South America**. Small pieces of bone found in **Argentina** belong to **Giganotosaurus** [gig-an-OH-toe-SORE-us]. This dinosaur is now thought to have been bigger and fiercer than T. rex and lived millions of years earlier. It possibly hunted the enormous **Argentinosaurus** [AR-gent-eeno-sore-us].

Europe is where the fossil remains of large dinosaur teeth were found by Mary and Gideon Mantell in England in 1822. They were the **first fossils** ever found of the dinosaur **Iguanodon** [ig-WHA-noh-don] (see pages 12-13).

Lots of dinosaur discoveries of the 20th and 21st centuries have been unearthed in **Asia**. **Jianianhualong** [Jee-an-yan-hoo-ah-long] is a slender **raptor** dinosaur that was covered in **feathers** and even had wings. It was first found in 2017 and scientists think it looked a bit like a chicken!

Europe

Asia

Africa

A fossil of the mighty **Spinosaurus** [SPINE-oh-SORE-us] was first found in the Sahara Desert in **Africa** in 1912.

In **Lesotho** in 1978, the first fossil of small and speedy **Lesothosaurus** [Le-SO-toe-sore-us] was uncovered.

Oceania

Dinosaurs that lived in **Antarctica** would have enjoyed a warmer climate than the icy weather the area is known for today. The continent would have been covered in trees, rather than ice, and home to dinosaurs such as **Cryolophosaurus** [cry-o-loaf-oh-sore-us] and the enormous Jurassic sauropod **Glacialisaurus** [glay-see-al-ee-SORE-us].

Dinosaur Cove in Victoria, **Australia** is another important dinosaur site. William Hamilton Ferguson discovered the first dinosaur fossil in Australia at the site in 1903. An almost complete skeleton of the dinosaur **Minmi** [min-me] was found there in 1989.

Antarctica

IGUANODON

Iguanodon was a large, plant-eating dinosaur that lived during the **Early Cretaceous** period. Iguanodon fossils have been found in many parts of the world.

First discovered: England, 1822

Discovered by:
Mary and Gideon Mantell

First fossil: Teeth

Fossils found around the world:
Belgium, England, USA

The first bones found were fossilised **teeth**. They looked similar to **iguana** teeth, but **ten times bigger**! Gideon Mantell thought the bones belonged to a giant prehistoric lizard, so he named this new creature Iguanodon. Experts disagreed and said the teeth belonged to a mammal, perhaps a rhinoceros!

Over the next 20 years, Gideon found **more teeth and bones.** Eventually he was able to **persuade** the experts that he was right — the bones did belong to a **giant prehistoric lizard** — a dinosaur!

Early drawings of Iguanodon show the dinosaur's **tail dragging** along the ground, like an **iguana's tail**. Now, experts think Iguanodon's heavy tail was **held stiffly** off the ground while the dinosaur walked on two or four legs.

Iguana

Iguanodon's **skull** was thin, tall and narrow. Its **eyes** were high on its head to help it see far and wide.

Iguanodon had a very long **tongue** and a flexible top **jaw**. As the lower jaw pressed into the top jaw, the top jaw could bend outwards to crush up food between its **teeth**.

Iguanodon had **four-fingered hands**. The three middle fingers were joined together by a piece of flesh but the fourth could move easily. The dinosaur's long spiky **thumb claw** is now its most famous feature.

Iguanodon had no **front teeth**, only a **beak** made from **keratin** – the same material as human **fingernails**. Its strong 5-cm-long back teeth could break down plant material easily.

Fossilised **track marks** found in England show Iguanodon walking on **two legs** (bipedal) but it's believed it could walk on **four legs** (quadrupedal) too. The dinosaur's ability to walk on two or four legs would have come in handy. Iguanodon may have found and eaten its food as it walked slowly on four legs but if it needed to **escape** a predator, it could get away quickly on its two longer back legs.

ANKYLOSAURUS

Ankylosaurus was another large plant-eating dinosaur from the **Late Cretaceous** period. Ankylosaurus was the largest of the **armoured** dinosaurs, called Ankylosaurids. No complete skeleton of this mighty dinosaur has been found — yet.

First discovered: Montana, USA, 1906

Discovered by: Barnum Brown

First fossils: Rib, bits of armour, part of a shoulder, sections of vertebrae and the top of a skull

Fossils found around the world: Canada, USA

Ankylosaurus was covered in **bony plates** and **scutes** and was built a bit like an armoured tank. Spikes ran down the length of its tail to meet its deadly **tail club**. The fossilised remains of two tail clubs have been found. Both are damaged, as though they had hit something hard, possibly when used for **defence**.

Ankylosaurus weighed up to **7,000 kg** and was **7 m** long. That's the length of an elephant.

Most Ankylosaurus **fossils** were fossilised **upside-down**. Dinosaur experts were keen to find out why. The most-likely answer is the **bloat and float theory**. The dinosaurs' bodies washed into rivers and seas, where they became bloated and eventually floated, before sinking to the bottom of the water.

The two Ankylosaurus **skulls** found so far each had large internal **sense organs**, so Ankylosaurus probably had a strong sense of **smell** to help it find food.

Ankylosaurus **skulls** were triangular with a narrow **beak** at the end and no sign of any grinding teeth. This meant Ankylosaurus could strip **leaves** from plants but it could not grind down large plant material.

Ankylosaurus was one of the **last dinosaurs**, living at the end of the Cretaceous period. Some experts have suggested its **armour** could be an **evolutionary** change that was slowly happening in plant-eating dinosaurs in order to **survive** in a world ruled by mighty meat-eaters, such as T. rex.

The partial **skeletons** reveal a large space where Ankylosaurus's **stomach** and **intestines** would have been. The space was probably very big to allow the dinosaur to **digest** the huge amount of **plant** material — about 60 kg — it needed to eat every day to support its size.

STEGOSAURUS

Stegosaurus was a large plant-eating dinosaur from the **Late Jurassic** period (155 to 145 mya). It could reach up to 6 m long, the size of a bus. It is famous for the **bony plates** that ran down its back and tail, making it seem even bigger than it was!

First discovered: USA, 1876

Discovered by: M.P. Felch and named by Othniel Charles Marsh in 1877

First fossil: Bone fragments

Fossils found around the world: USA

Stegosaurus had a bendy **tail** with **spikes** on the end, called **thagomizers**. They could be as long as a metre in length. Fossil finds of some of these spikes show **damage**, suggesting the dinosaur used them as a **weapon** to defend itself.

Scientists have also found thagomizer puncture **wounds** on the fossil remains of Stegosaurus's main **predator** - Allosaurus [AL-oh-sore-us].

The surfaces of the **plates** on Stegosaurus's back and tail were covered in tiny grooves where **blood vessels** might have been. This could suggest blood passed through the plates as a way of **cooling** the dinosaur down or **warming** it up.

Othniel Charles Marsh, the scientist who gave Stegosaurus its name, originally thought the **fossil bones** belonged to an animal that lived in **water**, like a turtle. He thought the dinosaur's bony plates lay flat on its back, a bit like the tiles on a roof.

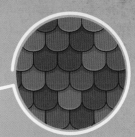

Discoveries of more complete skeletons led experts to realise that the bony **plates** stood **upright** in two **rows**, in an alternating pattern.

A space in the **hip** of early Stegosaurus fossils led scientists to think that Stegosaurus had a **brain** in its tail that controlled the lower half of its body. They wondered if it gave the dinosaur a burst of speed when under attack. Other experts quickly dismissed the theory of an extra brain in the dinosaur's bottom!

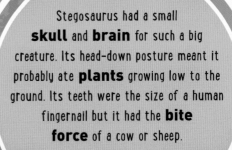

Stegosaurus had a small **skull** and **brain** for such a big creature. Its head-down posture meant it probably ate **plants** growing low to the ground. Its teeth were the size of a human fingernail but it had the **bite force** of a cow or sheep.

The most complete **skeleton** of Stegosaurus went on display in the Natural History Museum, London, UK, in 2014. Nicknamed 'Sophie', the exhibit is **85 per cent complete**, although her head is not real. The real skull is too delicate to display – it is made up of 50 tiny bones. The skeleton was found in 2003 in Wyoming, USA.

TRICERATOPS

Triceratops, with its three enormous **horns** and large **frill** around its head, is perhaps one of the most famous dinosaurs. This 9-m-long creature roamed Earth during the **Cretaceous** period about 66 million years ago.

First discovered:
USA, 1887

Discovered by: Unknown

First fossil: Partial horn

Fossils found around the world: North America

When the **first fossil** was found, it was thought that the bone came from a giant prehistoric **bison** and the animal was named *bison alticornis*. It was renamed Triceratops in 1889 after the palaeontologist John Bell Hatcher found the first Triceratops skull in 1888.

So far, more than **50 skulls** and some **partial skeletons** of Triceratops have been found, including the **skulls** of young Triceratops.

T. rex **bite marks** on Triceratops fossil bones show that this meat-eater managed to **feast** on Triceratops from time to time. That would have been quite a meal!

In 1997, a fossil was discovered with a **horn bitten off** and bite marks that belonged to a **T. rex**. The wounds had healed, which means that this Triceratops had successfully **fought off** an attack from a large meat-eating predator.

In 2017, builders found fossil bones of a Triceratops when working on a new fire and police station in Colorado, USA. Further digging revealed the main parts of the **skull**, both **horns** above the eyes and parts of its lower **jaw**. **Vertebrae**, ribs and a shoulder blade were also excavated from the same site.

The 2017 discovery was exciting because the **skull** of Triceratops is often found on its own. It is rare to find the skull alongside other bones. This is probably because once the dinosaur has died, the smaller parts of the body **decay** or get **eaten** by **scavengers**, but the strong skull bones stay around for a while.

There is **debate** amongst scientists as to whether **Triceratops** and another dinosaur **Torosaurus** [tor-oh-SORE-us] are in fact the same dinosaur. One expert has suggested that Torosaurus, whose **head frill** has large **holes** in it, is simply Triceratops in old age but other scientists disagree.

DIPLODOCUS

Diplodocus [DIP-low-DOCK-us] was a big sauropod that lived during the **Late Jurassic** period. Its **long neck** was useful when reaching for leaves high up in the trees, and experts think its long tail acted as a whip for defence.

There have been **lots** of **fossils** of Diplodocus found over the years, including some **near-complete skeletons**. Most Diplodocus fossils have been discovered in the Rocky Mountain area of Colorado, Montana, Utah and Wyoming in the USA.

First discovered: Colorado, USA, 1877

Discovered by: Benjamin Mudge and Samuel W. Williston

First fossil: Vertebrae and other bones

Fossils found around the world: USA

In the early 20th century, experts believed Diplodocus walked with **sprawled legs** like a crocodile or lizard. This theory was quickly disproven in the 1920s.

In the 1930s, fossil **footprints** suggested the dinosaur had four thick, strong **legs** that went **straight** down under its body and allowed it to move slowly, a bit like an **elephant**.

In 1905, a cast of a Diplodocus **skeleton** was given to the Natural History Museum in London. It was nicknamed 'Dippy'. It was originally displayed with its **tail** down but, in 1995, after **new research** showed that the tail would have been lifted up to balance the neck, Dippy's tail was raised up high. Dippy sometimes goes on tour around the UK.

In October 2018, scientists revealed that a **skull** found in 2010 in Montana, USA, belonged to a **juvenile** Diplodocus. Less than 12 Diplodocus skulls have been dug up to date so this tiny one, nicknamed 'Andrew', is a very **rare** discovery. It is just **25.5 cm** wide and experts think the dinosaur was less than **five years old** when it died.

Dippy is **cleaned** every two years. It takes two people two days to clean Dippy's **292 bones**.

Andrew's **skull** was found in a **bone bed** with at least 16 other similar juvenile dinosaurs. The bones are dotted with **mud**, which might suggest the dinosaur herd **died** in a **flood**.

Diplodocus's neck had **15 vertebrae** and it had a row of extra **bones** underneath its **spine**, which probably helped **support** the dinosaur's long **neck** and spine.

The **longest near-complete** dinosaur **skeleton** we have is of a Diplodocus. Other dinosaurs were bigger but we have not yet found a complete set of bones from these species.

VELOCIRAPTOR

Velociraptor was a fierce, turkey-sized dinosaur from the **Cretaceous** period. It was covered in **feathers** and had fearsome **claws** on its back feet that were used to stab its prey and prevent it from escaping.

Henry Fairfield Osborn was an American scientist who first described Velociraptor in 1924. He assumed the **fossilised claw** was from the dinosaur's **hand**. We now know it was the **second toe** of the dinosaur's foot.

First discovered: Gobi Desert, Mongolia, 1924

Discovered by: Henry Fairfield Osborn

First fossils: Claw and a crushed skull

Fossils found around the world: Mongolia and China

Velociraptor's **tail bones** were **fused together** so the tail was long and stiff to **help** it run, hunt and jump on its prey.

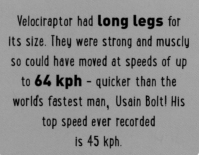

Velociraptor had **long legs** for its size. They were strong and muscly so could have moved at speeds of up to **64 kph** – quicker than the world's fastest man, Usain Bolt! His top speed ever recorded is 45 kph.

Experts have found **fossilised evidence** of how Velociraptor behaved. A famous fossil was found in 1971 that shows the dinosaur locked in a **battle** with a horned plant-eater called **Protoceratops** [pro-toe-serra-tops]. It is likely the pair died when a sandstorm or collapsing dune buried them in battle.

Another **rare** Velociraptor **fossil** was found in 2012. Inside the skeleton of the young Velociraptor was the **remains** of its last **meal** - the broken bone of a **pterosaur** [ter-oh-sore]. The **flying reptile** would have been too big and dangerous to hunt, so the dinosaur probably **scavenged** the bone from the creature after it had died.

Quill knobs are tiny bumps on the wing bones of some modern-day birds. They help hold flight **feathers** in place. The discovery of quill knobs on a Velociraptor fossil found in 2017 could prove that this dinosaur had long feathers that stretched over its arms.

Further evidence that Velociraptor had **feathers** can be found with its close relatives **Microraptor** [MIKE-roh-rap-tor] and **Zhenyuanlong** [Zen-yu-an-long]. Fossils of both of these dinosaurs have been found with feathers intact.

Despite its wing-like **feathered arms**, Velociraptor couldn't fly. It probably had feathers to keep it **warm**, for use during **mating displays** or to keep its **eggs warm**.

TYRANNOSAURUS REX

Tyrannosaurus rex is considered the ultimate **carnivore**. This famously fierce **predator** lived during the **Late Cretaceous** period and was one of the last of the dinosaurs.

First discovered: Hill Creek Formation, Montana, USA, 1902

Discovered by: Barnum Brown

First fossil: Fragments of bone

Fossils found around the world: North America

Barnum Brown discovered the first recognised fossils of T. rex in Montana, USA. Only **seven T. rex fossils** that are more than **half-complete** have been found since, but we still **know a lot** about this dinosaur.

Experts know T. rex was a fierce meat-eater because its **bite marks** have been found on the fossil bones of **Triceratops** and **Edmontosaurus** [ed-MON-toe-sore-us].

T. rex was up to **12 m long** and its enormous **7,000 kg** weight meant it could take on **large prey**, such as Triceratops.

Coprolites (see pages 8–9) from T. rex revealed these dinosaurs weren't too fussy – they didn't just eat flesh but **crunched through bone** too.

In 2013, a study described the finding of a **T. rex tooth** in the **tailbone** of a duckbilled dinosaur. The bone had **healed** over the tooth, suggesting the **prey** had got away, taking a bit of its predator with it!

T. rex is known for its **short arms** and scientists still **debate** what the dinosaur used these for. Could they **grasp** struggling **prey** or help the dinosaur get up and down from the ground? Perhaps they had **no function**, like the wings of **flightless birds** today, such as an ostrich.

Studies of fossils show that T. rex's **bite force** meant it could easily bite through **bone**. In 1996, scientists described one fossil of a **Triceratops** pelvis that was covered in more than **50 T. rex bite marks**!

Some scientists have suggested a T. rex's **arms** were more **useful** when it was a **juvenile**. Its short arms would have been more in **proportion** with the rest of its **body** and may have been helpful when **hunting** or **scavenging** prey. As the dinosaur grew, it didn't need to use its arms to hunt or find food.

In 2014, scientists may have found the **trackways** of three tyrannosaurs in Canada. They appear to have been moving in the **same direction** at the **same time**. These individuals may have been **living** as a group or even **hunting** as a **pack**. One animal was missing a **claw** from its left foot, which may have been a **battle wound**.

SPINOSAURUS

Spinosaurus was one of the **largest meat-eating dinosaurs** ever. It was up to 18 m long and weighed around 4,000 kg. It was thinner than T. rex, with longer forearms and a huge sail-like structure on its back. It had a long snout with large, sharp pointed teeth.

First discovered: Egypt 1911-1914

Discovered by: Ernst Stromer

First fossil: Two partial skeletons

Fossils found around the world:
Morocco, Egypt

The first, and most complete, Spinosaurus bones were found in the **Sahara Desert** in Egypt. The fossils were **displayed** in a museum in **Munich** in Germany but the building was **bombed** during the **Second World War** (1939-45) and the fossils were **destroyed**. All that was left were a few drawings, Stromer's field notes and some photographs.

In 2013, palaeontologist Nizar Ibrahim and his team **rediscovered** Spinosaurus in the Sahara. Using **digital technology**, experts **reconstructed** Spinosaurus from the fossil remains of a skull, claws and bones that formed the dinosaur's famous back sail.

The **fossil bones** looked like they belonged to an animal that lived in the water. They were **dense**, like the bones of **manatees** and **dugongs**, both aquatic animals. This density would have helped the dinosaur to **float**. Its sail might also have helped it to **swim**.

This **discovery** and research led scientists to believe that Spinosaurus was possibly the **first dinosaur** that had **adapted** to **life** in the **water**. Its back legs were shorter than other predators of the time and its claws were wide, making its feet almost paddle-shaped.

Ibrahim may have also discovered what these dinosaurs **ate**. Spinosaurus' teeth could interlock inside its long snout, like a **crocodile's**, to **catch fish**. Maybe Spinosaurus was a **fish-eater** too!

DINOSAUR DETECTIVES

Palaeontologists are scientists who study fossils. There have been many famous dinosaur fossil hunters over the years. Here are some of them!

OTHNIEL CHARLES MARSH (1831–1899) AND EDWARD DRINKER COPE (1840–1897)

During the Great Dinosaur Rush in USA, these two men discovered over 150 species in their fight to be the best dinosaur hunter. This battle, called the Bone Wars, lasted until Cope's death in 1897. But the pair did make a few mistakes along the way. Marsh publicly humiliated Cope by revealing he had placed the head of Elasmosaurus on its tail! The famous battle lost both men their fortunes but science learned much from their numerous discoveries.

MARY ANNING (1799–1847)

Mary and her family hunted for fossils on the beaches of England and sold them to wealthy tourists. She discovered many famous dinosaurs and prehistoric creatures, including Iguanodon and Ichthyosaur, but because she was poor and a woman, nobody paid much attention to her work. Today, we recognise Anning as an important palaeontologist in her own right.

BARNUM BROWN (1873-1963)

Barnum Brown spent most of his adult life hunting for fossils around the world. He was the first scientist to find a partial skeleton of Tyrannosaurus rex and would later find a more complete specimen that would form the basis for our understanding of this famous dinosaur.

DONG ZHIMING (1937-)

Dong Zhiming is a leading palaeontologist in China and around the world. He made his first dinosaur fossil find at 26. It was a vertebra from a sauropod, the most gigantic of dinosaurs to have walked the Earth. He has since uncovered many dinosaurs in China and named about 20 dinosaurs himself.

PATRICIA VICKERS-RICH (1944-)

Patricia and her husband Tim Rich have uncovered many dinosaurs in Australia's Dinosaur Cove - such as Leaellynasaura and Timimus, both named after their children. Her work has helped prove that some dinosaurs could survive in the very cold conditions of Cretaceous Australia - a very different climate to today!

DR KAREN CHIN

Dr Chin is an American palaeontologist who is one of the world's leading experts on coprolites. Studying coprolites enables her to look for evidence of feeding habits and behaviour and to discover the diets of ancient creatures, including the dinosaurs.

GLOSSARY

adapted changed for a new purpose

armour tough layer that some plants and animals have for protection

bone bed an area of land that contains the bones of animals

Cretaceous period a period in Earth's history, between 144 and 65 mya

decay to rot

digest to break down food in the stomach

dune a mound of sand formed by the wind

evolutionary the process by which animals and plants have developed and adapted during the history of Earth

excavated dug up

fossilisation the process of fossilising an animal or plant that once lived

frill a fringe of feather or bony plates around an animal's head

iguana a tropical lizard

Jurassic period a period of Earth's history, between 206 and 144 mya

juvenile a young animal

Mesozoic Era a period of time in Earth's history when the dinosaurs lived

palaeontologist a scientist who studies fossils

Pangaea the supercontinent that existed on Earth before it broke apart into smaller continents

plates thin, flat areas that form a structure

predator an animal that eats other animals

preserve to keep something as it is

pterosaur a flying reptile from the Mesozoic era

reconstruct rebuild or make again after something has been damaged or destroyed

sandstorm a strong wind that carries clouds of sand with it, often in a desert

sauropods a group of dinosaurs that walked on four legs, had long tails and necks, small heads and thick, column-shaped limbs

scavenger an animal that feeds on dead plants or animals

scutes thickened bony plates on the back of an animal

sediment soft matter that settles on the surface of the land or on the seabed, and over time may form into rock

species a group of animals which are closely related to one another

thagomizer an arrangement of spikes on the tails of some dinosaurs

theropod a group of meat-eating dinosaurs

vertebrae the bones that make up the spine of an animal

X-ray a photographic image of the inside of something, especially a body

FURTHER INFORMATION

Further Reading

Curious about Fossils by Kate Waters (Grosset and Dunlap, 2016)

Dictionary of Dinosaurs: an illustrated A to Z of every dinosaur ever discovered by Dr Matthew G. Baron (Wide Eyed Editions, 2018)

The Bone Wars: Clash of the Dinosaur Hunters by Nicky Dee (Dragonfly Group, 2017)

History VIPs: Mary Anning by Kay Barnham (Wayland, 2016)

Prehistoric Life series by Clare Hibbert (Franklin Watts, 2019)

Websites

www.nationalgeographic.com/science/2018/09/photos-dinosaurs-fossils-t-rex-triceratops-velociraptor-paleontology/

www.dkfindout.com/uk/dinosaurs-and-prehistoric-life/fossils/

www.nationalgeographic.com/science/prehistoric-world/fossil-wars/

www.nhm.ac.uk/discover/how-to-draw-a-dinosaur.html

INDEX

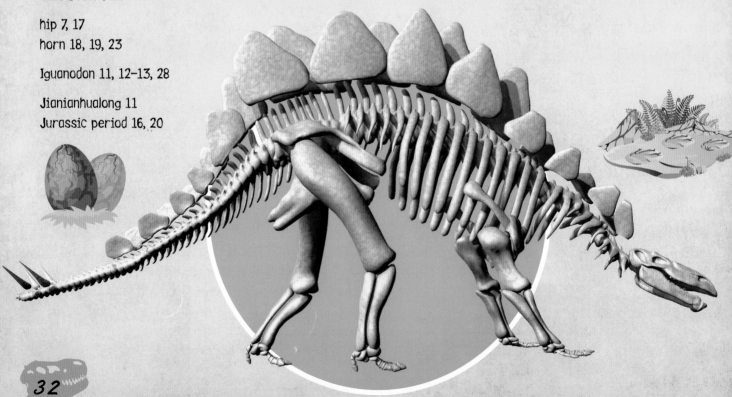

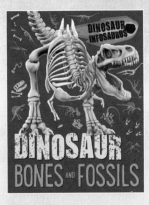

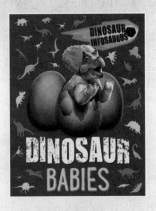

DINOSAUR INFOSAURUS

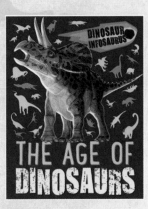